In Full Velvet

In Full Velvet

Poems

Jenny Johnson

SARABANDE BOOKS · LOUISVILLE, KY

Library of Congress Cataloging-in-Publication Data

Names: Johnson, Jenny, 1979- author.
Title: In full velvet / Jenny Johnson.
Description: Louisville, KY : Sarabande Books, 2017. | Includes
bibliographical references and index.
Identifiers: LCCN 2016014117 (print) | LCCN 2016027029 (ebook) | ISBN
9781941411377 (hardback) | ISBN 9781941411384
Subjects: | BISAC: NATURE / Ecology. | SOCIAL SCIENCE / Gender Studies. |
SOCIAL SCIENCE / Feminism & Feminist Theory.
Classification: LCC PS3610.O3564 A6 2017 (print) | LCC PS3610.O3564 (ebook) |
DDC 811/.6—dc23
LC record available at https://lccn.loc.gov/2016014117

Interior and exterior design by Kristen Radtke.

Manufactured in Canada.
This book is printed on acid-free paper.

Sarabande Books is a nonprofit literary organization.

This project is supported in part by an award from the National Endowment for the Arts. The Kentucky
Arts Council, the state arts agency, supports Sarabande Books with state tax dollars and federal funding
from the National Endowment for the Arts.

Contents

1

Dappled Things

Thank you day for dappled things—
      For ambrosia beetles streaking skylines inside a maple
For pansies speckled as a painter's sleeve
      For russet-crusted sidewalks of lichen, airy springs
of fiery-structured fringe For pink corpuscles
      making midges soon to burst out the undersides of leaves

Thank you for all that's still somehow
      counter, original, spare, and strange
For the brightening swell of a honeybee's sting
      For the alien markings on my girlfriend's cheek and how
         they form a perfect triangle

Thank you for the risen stars on the skin of an apple,
      which I slice into fine, thin crescents
For dapple is a word derived from apple
      and apple once meant any fruit at all
born from a tree: lemon, fig, persimmon
      Thank you road apple, finger apple, earth apple

for all that apple was before apple acquired
      a stigma for being forbidden—
Marked, dappled, shadowed grappling,
      stamped juice, controlled smudging of
          what twinkles unthinkably

And because I'm minion this morning to gay old music
Thanks Gentle Hop for this this-ness, for teaching attention
How to mark hard word-bodies with stress,
acute glyphs, blue scores For reckoning the risks
in discipline's rod—between sheets of loose-leafed linen—
You knew few might hear your coded address

Do I look hard enough to receive?
I am not moved by God, but I am moved by this
To experience the largesse: *What you look hard at seems*
to look hard at you O to be marked reciprocally, yes please
Across, above, below and with

I kiss my hand to male bonobos making out in public
  in spite of Western science
trying to explain away The glorious kink
  of spinner dolphins' whistle-clicks
over-under rolling, belly-on-belly clasping by the soft tips
  of flukes, riding dorsal rudders to the brink

I am inspired, call my girlfriend, say: Won't you be my Olympic marmot
  chewing on my ear till I lift my tail?
My black-billed magpie babble-singing to my begging call?
  My lioness, growl, thrust, roll on backs afterward?
    Squeaky as killer whales

We could keep contact relentless before
        the next sequence, diving deep in a reversed-role
double-helix formation, splashing swagger
        to reveal the length of our pink organs Or
we could be lady elephants heading down to the watering hole,
        gearing up to gather friends in the yard

for a yipp-purr chorus, hammerhead stork pile-up Or Love
        we could pretend to be utter strangers!
I, a house sparrow, and you, a cowbird, hopping over to chatter
        until you touch your lower bill, head bowed
                            to my breast feathers

Our days are charged by so much nature—
        The succulents we carry to Alexis in a plastic bag after her surgery
A cat pawing at a mantis behind a windowpane
        What we didn't wash from the lettuce, dirt that's good danger
Not pristine, not a baseline to harken after romantically
        Instead, I read that snowy cities should ready for rising heat, harder rain

Have I come to terms with dominance—what I have trammeled
        and fogged with my breath? Flush cut, a redesigned ecology
The dead won't say how the forest was before we came
        And the pheromones I bury my face in under your arms
                        make me a hazy archaeologist

I must speak of erasure when I long to be leaf-whelmed,
        lit by fire pinks and wild sweet Williams How dare
I speak of the marked when I am the diurnal creature damming
        the night sky with engineered lights We've generated a realm
where we can always see, never see From an aerial
        view, here's my bright address—refracting, scram-

-bling, shutting out the dark O day in the Anthropocene
        when I go to pull up buttercups, bare-
fingered, so I can better reach the runners, thin-rooted trams
        tunneling invasively Where's Hope? Hope's a weed, obscene
                on my head, springing white hairs

Like an extinct frog who brought life by opening her mouth,
    many froglets bursting out, I brood A quiet storm
at the water's edge, a bloated cloud, all the roe I've swallowed whole
    I brood and brood, feeling old Hop in his final state
crying out, *I am gall, I am heartburn*
    Until I feel a blaze unknown

Feel first my lungs deflate, then like a sharpening harp
    the stomach acids start to transform
I'm breathing through my skin, as an army grows in full
    Will all things return—if I so choose to burp—
        in nameless forms?

Come second heartbeat sounding in the breast
Come prismatic light dissembling
Come familiar spirit Come bare-chested in the weeds
Come private imposter Come hidden ballast
Come sudden departures Come stress without shape
Because belief is odd Come swaggering answer
Come invisible ink Come beatific scrawl
Come as squirrels are climbing backwards
Come as dogwood blossoms come apart
Come strumming an unspeakable power ballad
Through a torrent of rain with cheeks flushed scarlet
Come down the rusty metal slide
Come belted kingfisher flapping
Come lavender asters wheeling
Come loose, a sapling lengthening
Come honeysuckle Come glistening

Tail

I picture the shameful length of it poking along behind me as I walk down
    Fifth Avenue, the odd sheen of it, shimmering in shop windows,
How after too many beers, I'd lumber back into bed, its strangeness
    between my legs.

But as the sun rises—the clean stretch, aesthetic vertebrae—how I might flex its
    elegant, careful weight.
Consider my newfound balance, how gracefully I ascend a flight of stairs,
    teetering on one leg, my rump poised just so!
Or how I might signal to my lover, wave fondly to her through the air,
    lift my fur to tickle her mouth, dash a small crumb off her lips.
In a midnight alley, flashing my snowy underside like a switchblade, we'd sprint
    through underbrush.
Had I a tail, I would be luminous and lingering as a comet, who traces the starry night
    with a broken ellipsis . . .

      *

As a kid, I remember the small green bubble inside the carpenter's level,
How it would dart from corner to corner,

And how good it felt to straddle the sawhorse, out behind the shed, half tomboy,
    half centaur,
How I clenched a two-by-four between my thighbones and it was part of me.

A nest of yellow jackets rose from beneath the splinters and, forgetting how to move,
    how to cry, how to run,
I let them sting and sting and sting, eleven times, leaving swells on my arms, neck, legs,
    feet, and shoulders.

★

O Lord of Parts, O Holy Tool Shed!
When I rise from these sore bones,
Look what you've taken, what you've left me—

In Full Velvet

When Aristotle dissected the embryos in bird eggs,
he mistook the spinal cord for the heart.

Anaximander of Miletus wrote that the first humans
burst out of the mouths of fish

and that we took form there
and were held prisoners until puberty.

At its root, taxidermy means to arrange skin.
O Love, how precise is any vision?

*

Gut a body and we're nothing left but pipes whistling in the breeze.
That's all the cassowary is when you slit her open:

She's lungs wrapped in dark fur. She's a full baritone with a soft wattle.
There's nothing in her casque but soft tissue.

Because it makes me want to turn away,
I watch film footage of scientists

poking through the pink tendons,
the reptilian claw of the euthanized *Casuarius*.

When they fondle the sweet spot, a talon shoots out and stabs a melon
the same as it would the appendix of a lazy zookeeper.

I had to cover my eyes when they severed the ancestral wing.

*

Before the antlers fall away, here's what
the taxidermist teaches:

Because the velvet grows onto the hide we have to skin it and cut it,
so nothing rips up and causes damage.

Being cautious that we don't give it a big yank,
use your knife and just kind of pull gently.

Go on—tap the skin away from the bur.
See we boned it out.

For hard boned deer we usually just kind of
but we can't do that when it's in full velvet or it will, you know.

Now we're going to put a puncture in the tip.
So, we're not just hitting the one vein.

That's what we want to see.

*

It's also true that some whitetails never lose their velvet.
Hunters raise their eyebrows calling them atypical,

antlered does, cactus bucks, monsters, shirkers,
ghosts, raggedy-horn freaks, because they lead

long solitary lives, unweathered
by the rutting season, because their antlers

are covered permanently in a skin
that most bucks shed in late summer,

because their velvet horns spike and slope
backwards, never hardening to pure bone,

growing ever more askew. A recent one slayed
at thirty points was described as having

stickers, kickers, and a whole lot of extra junk
full of blood, hot to the human touch.

★

When talking about how the brain imagines the body,
neurologists use the word "schema" to describe the little map

that lies across the cortex, sensing
all our visible and invisible parts.

Love, we are more than utility, I think.

Some phantasms about our bodies in relationship to gender and sexuality
are idealized, some degrading, some compulsory, some transgressive.

Love, I know my body's here when the turkey vulture comes out of the thicket,
wings spread wide, smelling all of it.

★

This embrace, Love, will keep us here in this perceptual field.

When I focus my binoculars, Love, I am as careful as a raccoon working its way

through trash. A soda can passes as the skull of a bird, an eyehole where somebody

drank some sugar down. Love, come close. Love, lie back. Love, lie with me here

beneath a bridge where the light falling on the water shimmers upward casting

shadows on the slats beneath. When you are here, Love, I am beside myself.

★

If secrets are prayers
then maybe bodies

are worth revealing
worth repeating

How much plumage
dare I show How much down

Some days I am rich
as the common garter snake

with more testosterone
than you can handle

and the sweetest stench
of pheromones

O small pouch O tiny nipple
O lactating man

Or as the French say *cyprine*
O Icelandic clam

And whales with lady hips
And dandelions in the thick grass

growing stamens growing pistils
O lion's tooth However the wind

rips each part apart However we
clone and clone and clone

The Bus Ride

When she turns from the window and sees me
she is as lovely as a thrush seeing for the first time all sides of the sky.

Let this be a ballet without intermission: the grace of this ride beside her
on the green vinyl, soft thunderclaps in the quarry.

Let me be her afternoon jay,
hot silo, red shale crumbling—

In the Dream

I was alone in a dyke bar we'd traversed before
or maybe it was in a way all our dives

merging together suddenly as one intergalactic composite,
one glitter-spritzed black hole,

one cue stick burnished down to a soft blue nub.
Picture an open cluster of stars

managing to forever stabilize in space
without a landlord scheming to shut the place down.

Anyways, I was searching for someone there
whom we hadn't seen in years—in what

could have been Sisters, Babes, the Lex, the Pint,
the Palms, or the E Room? —but the room

had no end and no ceiling.
Though I could see all of our friends or exes

with elbows up or fingers interlocked
on tabletops zinging with boomerangs.

Maybe the tables were spinning, too. I can't be sure.
But just as a trap that trips before

hammering a mouse is not humane
the dream changed—or the alarm

that I carry in my breast pocket in my waking life
was sounding. Because in the dream

three people on bar stools, who were straight
or closeted? but more importantly angry

turned and the room dwindled
like a sweater full of moths eating holes

through wool. Or they were humans, sure,
but not here to love

with jawlines set to throw epithets like darts
that might stick or nick or flutter past

as erratically as they were fired.
You could say their hostility was a swirl

nebulous as gas and dust,
diffuse as the stress

a body meticulously stores.
Like how when I was shoved in grade school

on the blacktop in my boy jeans
the teacher asked me if I had a strawberry

because the wound was fresh as jam, glistening
like pulp does after the skin of a fruit is

peeled back clean with a knife.
I was in the dream as open to the elements,

yet I fired back. And I didn't care who eyed me
like warped metal to be pounded square.

I said: *Do you realize where you are?*

And with one finger I called our family forth
and out of the strobe lights, they came.

Severe

|sə'vi(ə)r| adj. unsparing, difficult, disciplined

By way of illustration, a storm, a hairdo, a punishment,
or the face of my great-aunt in the failing memory
of the few who can snap her cool features into place.

Overheard usage: The old maid, hair cropped unfashionably short
in mannish trousers, how else to describe her but severe.

       Like Joan of Arc suited to ride,
her chain mail shimmering, iridescent as a tarpon
lunging from an angler's tackle, a hook dangling
by a wire.

       Maybe it's genetic,
the clean line of my jaw in the blue porch light.
What if I nick your finger, punish you like
a paper cut, or kiss you with desire's accuracy,
I mean, the way a skater's blade etching a figure eight
kisses the ice?

As if to be butch is to be made of mythical perimeters,
and not the sky revealing itself between storms
in sudden naked flashes.

I found my great-aunt's face in a grainy yearbook photo,
absent of restraint, a playful eyebrow raised, a smile so
genteel and at her ear, a blonde helix, stray curl almost
too exceptionally soft for sight.

Elegy at Twice the Speed of Sound

At fifteen I was so willing to wait it out underground

I cut practice to disappear beneath the pavement, carrying only a flashlight
      in the waistband of my nylon track shorts,

a red trace of graffiti beckoning me forward through a strange and drafty tunnel—
      sometimes I moved through it with my hands,

sliding my body over a sudden slant of slick concrete, until one dark crawl space
      opened into another and another.

As each car passed above, a sliver of light from a manhole would wink shut.
      Was I vanishing?

Instead of returning? Eyes wincing open in disbelief at a woman,
      who waves to me now in a faded T-shirt
      from the front stoop of her apartment complex.

How long was I under? And who rescued me?

At a cocktail party after work, a small girl runs through adult legs.

She ducks beneath a chair, spying my every move,
      watching the way I furrow my brow or tilt my head back to laugh.

    *

I should sprint ahead, but instead I vomit in the chalked lines of a football field
      swaying back and forth until all the parallels blur into one
      and I see for the first time the waste of my adolescence—

I should shake my friend, who forgets who he *is*
        after too many shots of bourbon, the flashing strobe,
        and a merciless skyline of shirtless men.

Or I should name this ache, call it archive fever, reading a speech
        given in 1992 by a man,
        (Why haven't I heard of him until now?)

a translator, a scholar, a poet, who warned before dying
        of complications from AIDS,
        "I will be somewhere listening for my name . . ."

Or should I go by what's been said of my elders, however little?
        Without a record, they were two "old maids."

And in 1989 when Peg was 68 and Dorothy 77, they flew
        to Paris on the Concorde at twice the speed of sound

to celebrate anniversaries that were not their own:
        D-day, the French Revolution, and the birth of the Eiffel Tower.

They were never two "old maids"

                                falling onto a bed at the local Y.

            Dorothy thinking herself cosmopolitan in her black beret.
            Peg in her skirt suit, electric with passion and temper.

                    Shoes kicked off, one lies back as the other

                        helps to slip off the day's stiff garments.
                    First the eyes and hooks unfastened, then each

> nylon stocking shimmied down the knee,
> peeled off the foot, before the startling relief, sweet

> gleam of skin, of a body surviving time
> still in mint condition, now lifted in soft light like a rare

> coin from its sleeve.

In my palm, a copper penny still gleaming.

And my lover with a look of mischief walking closer.

And Melvin Dixon too exhausted to translate Senghor, while hearing a voice,
  suddenly, lovingly *calling his name.*

And Peg dragging her schnauzer out for an evening walk.

And Dorothy ordering a steak well done.

And a small girl with eyes bent on a rerun of *Robin Hood*,
  longing to vanish in the forest,
    drops her knife at the kitchen table to announce, *Call me Bow.*

*

Where there is
no lineage, no record,
no quantifiable
proof, there are
myths, and where
there are no myths,
there are traces:

*

Ready at last for our rendezvous across the Atlantic?

Don't worry. Soon we'll be there.
Two old dames storming the Bastille.

Of course, I didn't forget to bring them.
Peg, how could I?

You've never in all these years let me forget a thing.
Need a pillow? Lift your head. There.

I think I feel it.
A change in pressure.

When the engine starts to accelerate,
when we reach Mach 2
we won't hear a thing.

As the droop nose angles
the delta wings slice through.
As the sun moves backwards,
our conveyance outrunning it,
we'll leave a thick white hole in the sky.

We'll leave a blast, a crack,
a boom, my dear.
A boom.

Dorothy's Trash:

No dog-eared copy of *The Price of Salt*,

no nude drawings from a community art class,

no painstakingly Kinseyan inventories,

no anagram tucked in a world atlas

where the Tapajós and Amazon rivers meet,

no souvenir (stucco wasp nest?) legible as the one

Miss Bishop left, no ticket stubs,

no letter typed in future perfect:

You will have to lift the shag carpet beneath the oak dresser.

There you will find a key; use it to open:

no love letters, no ashes to say

the letters were burned.

Not much here: an empty canvas bought for $1.35

still wrapped in cellophane, a bottle

of turpentine too hazardous to dispose of,

Life magazines, a lone wolf spider, some expired meds.

Like I said, nothing here,

and me now, on hands and knees

to sniff around, to root behind,

to put one fist deep in the compost

just to feel the heat

of matter breaking down.

There Are New Worlds

To ride a horse is holy.
Like how Stephen refusing to ride sidesaddle
in *The Well of Loneliness*

fully astride, rides high on
the acrid sweat
of leather.

On the overleaf of my worn copy,
there by the pond, next to Stephen
isolated on a stone, is a swan.

I first kissed a woman
after hours of silence and shared cherry Chap Stick
late at night on a bench

in a garden that was so historical
Thomas Jefferson must have sat there, too
cross-legged in his wig

or Gertrude Stein, I hope, legs straddled wide
on a speaking tour
explaining, *A rose is a rose is a rose*

I strode home alone
cutting through
the icy November chill

like a cygnet paddling
suddenly
in a fresh, dark lake.

Altitudes

Pressed against a pinball machine, a finger slips

down, down your blue button-down

taps your chest. Granite cliff face, oh El

Capitan. And in the blur of champagne

you fear looking up! Try and kiss her steady

nipple, promise the impossible and gravity

will drop. Here her hand hovers

a cirrus cloud above Mount Tam,

city tilting, slippage on the steering wheel.

Below: rush hour miniature on Market,

thin outlines of gulls plumbing

Ocean Beach, Castro signage blinking

in pink. You are so much higher now

than on tiptoes before a mirror

wetting your hair down, fixated on

the asymmetry of a part. You strained

in the mirror for a backdrop like this—

where a guide at your ear says, *keep climbing*

2

Souvenirs

*

The boots of the dead poet were size 11,
licorice black with a stitch of blue up the calf.
Without the long legs that once filled them,
sent them scuffing through the San Joaquin Valley,
they slouch on an oak pedestal in the university library
next to a white placard that tells an anecdote
about the writer's irreverence at staff meetings,
his casual drop of the f-bomb. Standing this close
I wonder if my ogling is offending him,
or if he might nudge me, gently,
longing to make a joke out of the strangeness of the scene,
look at how absence blinds us
to the scale of our attachments.

*

At the small funeral, a woman lifts her camera,
toggles the zoom button and begins
taking pictures of her mother's hands
in a casket, draped across a polyester dress.
When someone asks her why
she is doing it, she mentions
the macramé, the doll parts, the needlepoint,
all the things her mother used to do
with *those* hands.
Someone sitting beside me
wanted to stop her then, beg her
to sit down, to leave the body be.

*

I loved a woman who curated loss.
She was a sculptor. After we had parted
in rage at the corner of 16th and Dolores,
after our old bed frame slid off the car roof,
splinters flurrying down I-80, after I'd moved
thousands of miles away, she called to ask if
she might build out of sugar cubes a replica of my house.
She said, for herself, she needed to see it
but didn't know the measurements.
I cannot explain my consent
that evening, alone, at home,
the yellow tape unspooling, I measured closet widths,
calculated the feet between hedges—
I wanted her to craft it perfectly to scale.

Eagle Lake

I drink you down
a swimmer's gulp of
waves, fen, and channel,
fallen pine needles like
thin spinning batons,
loose rhizomes sticking
between teeth, spatterdocks
leaving their brandy back
wash, even the diluted
fuel blathering out the
back end of a fisherman's
boat with a painted sign
that reads: "Bite Me." We wave
acknowledging our human
presence in this basin, too.
As dragonflies attach
acrobatically above
and the lanceolate leaves
of the flame azaleas along
the shoreline shiver in the
wind, I drink what I need,
head tipped as a loon whose
red eyes establish a target
before cruising deep.
Amid so much glassy motion
am I carrying what neighbors
warn of—a beaver fever
passed downstream?
I drink amid nurse logs
dripping with effervescent
moss, tannins in the soil

beneath the hemlocks seeping
into runnels around my feet,
my shirt front wet as
a flooding fall gushing
with matter and methyl-
mercury and other unnamable
compounds that have traveled
from smokestacks states away,
as if my skin were permeable
enough to absorb particles
misting us during a morning rain
and my mouth an old spring house
on a hillside holding onto
whatever bubbles up—

Pine Street Barbershop

Sliding back in the basin, I let him
rub my skull, rinse

the eucalyptus suds out of my ears,
wrap my tee in a great black cape,

ask without needing an answer:
The usual? Captain of this noonday helm,

Cupid stands tall on an apple crate,
a lift from which he reaches to snip

every stray, wet pinch of hair.
Since last I visited, his stubble

filled in, a close neat beard. Eyeing
the hem of my Levi's,

he says he's been searching
for a suit, bespoke for someone

our size. Says he's found a shop that'll
tailor him a jacket made of wool

Italian milled, Bemberg lining
with a notched lapel.

We speak through the mirror;
the glass is larger than we are.

In it I see my father, rubbing
his head dry with a towel,

whispering softly to my mother:
Which tie? Lost in his undershirt,

unsure how to proceed.
Where would you wear it? I ask.

Everywhere, Cupid says. Dipping his shears
in a jar of blue Barbicide,

he drifts; I follow him out the door
into a streaming metropolis of

masculinities vested in
tweed, plaid, velvet, seersucker,

surgeon's cuffs unbuttoned.
Bound like backstitches

and long staple cotton, we level
suede elbows. We promenade

through Southern streets. We alter
nothing. We alter everything.

Gay Marriage Poem

We could promise to elope
like my grandmother did
if a football team won

on homecoming night.
We could be good queers?
An oxymoron we never

longed for. We could
become wed-*locked*
as the suffix was once intended:

laiko, Common Teutonic for play,
not *loc,* Old English for a cave,
an enclosure. Instead

of a suit, I could wear my T-shirt
that avows, "Support Your Right
to Arm Bears!" Or we could

wed in bear suits
just as I saw people do
one summer in San Francisco

standing amid a grassy median
during rush hour.
They were so personally

anonymously political
blocking the ocean breeze
in acrylic fur.

Forget such solemnities!
I want to run through streets
shouting up to all my beloveds' windows:

Friends! In sickness and in health
I refuse to forsake you!
on Charlotte Street, Home,

Euclid, Decatur, Union,
Straubs, Rebecca, Bennett Ave.,
38th, Woolslayer Way.

In the only wedding I was a part of
I was the flower girl
who held up the ceremony

kneeling to drop equal dividends of
petals beside every pew,
refusing to leave anyone out.

Let us speak without occasion
of relations of our choosing!
Tied intricately

as the warps and wefts
amid mats of moss,
without competing for sunlight

our hairy caps are forever
lodging in spaces
that myopic travelers can't see.

Of such loves unwrit, at the boundary layer
between earth and air,
I feel most clear.

Folsom Street Fairytale

Once upon a time her cheeks were Popsicle red and the leather a licorice twist.

Once upon a time she swung you like a cub by your scruff.

Once upon a time clamped nipples like twin satellites.

Once upon a time whatever she strapped on turned into a swan.

Bent over in studded chaps, she could be anyone:

the next-door neighbor, a hockey mom, a public defender,

the bank teller with those long lashes.

My grandma always told me if life gives you lemons
throw 'em away. And so, we loosen. Shuffle off sore tendons.

Mondays. Insults catcalled out Chevy windows.
Clinking whiskey glasses, we wipe away sweat and old flames.

All I ever found in the gravel was the paper body,
what the garter snake shed. Take off that old suit, tonight.

Even as your good arm shudders to the mat, like the moon
meeting the mouth of the Shenandoah. Take off that old suit.

In new skin, come back again and again. Own this acreage,
this new ground rippling under rolled sleeves.

Little Apophat

Your child is a little lion cub
ready to tear into
a hunk of antelope is
a fuse bursting into
electric sprays of light
is trouble, you
say, like me. Has
your eyes though, pale
as the eggs of quail.

Yes. And also, shouting
No! as I reach for her balled fist
I wonder if she is
our negative capability.
Dare I say she's beautiful
or that seeing another photo
I feel inexplicably like a father
though I am nothing other
than an ex-girlfriend
falling in and out of touch?

I like to study
not her features exactly,
but all her small perfect shadows.
Her sleeves like swallow's wings,
the oblong ring she casts
moving down a slide,
some latent echo inside you
now there of me, some remnant
of the night we longed to
against the drum of a water tower,

but did it instead again and again
on a bed too small for one.

Would it stretch wonder
if all our immaterial actions
could sire the ambition that ignites
when we let a child sit
too long with her own design,
let her stack blocks
one cube at a time, sturdy as
a well-pointed chimney
or a giraffe's dorsal spine
or a tower of solid cheerleaders
kneeling into sweaty backs and thighs,
until the pyramid's gotten too high
and without warning
all the bodies tumble down,
laughing.

★

Little Nothing,
dare I tell you
what your mother and I made?

Firsts and fights
that left the kitchen
whitened by a fine silt of flour
and bras twisted into
the untidy nests of lyrebirds
and closety love
at the drunken end of straight parties,
in cemeteries
and in shower stalls.

Without sheet music
we were prodigious,
learning by ear and mouth
how to produce
each vocal score,
and when we were done
and we felt like making more,
we made it. And we made
sweet, fast nothings
with other people, too.

Little Apophat,
I could tell you stories of
scientific miracles,
late ovulation in garter snakes,
the courting rituals of macaques
playing hide and seek
behind tree trunks,
how when seals stay out to sea
months after mating
biologists call all that waiting
suspended animation.

Which is to say that
making you took time.

Fish Out of Water

As cars pull in the lot behind the old warehouse
kicking up gravel to make a U-turn

and a perched grackle wings its way
toward a branch, close enough that I can see

the feathers spiked roughly beneath the beak,
an iridescent weight making limbs sway,

I sit on the bank of the Missouri
not knowing where else to be.

The muddy river seems still almost
except for the places where it whorls.

Every few minutes a fish flips itself into the air
and then splashes beneath the surface,

something I can't catch, but try to—
the tattoo on your right arm, the moth there

in motion. You work by moving things
into positions, by reversing a scrap of paper,

by pasting your body hair beneath the text:
Getting Down to Business. Yesterday, a piece of

oblong fabric—a wobbly presence—
belonged here, floating about the frame.

And today, what could be
the arms of a cactus

makes more sense by itself.
Each shape is revealed by the spaces

in-between. Rolled together in the night
you weren't sure how to speak at first of

your body's position to mine
but then you could.

The small-town heat makes everything stick,
our skin pressing into one another,

the hair soft and light above your tailbone—
I won't forget how you directed me there.

Spaces

I do not know how
she felt, but I keep

thinking of her—
screaming out to an empty street.

I had been asleep
when I heard a voice

screaming, *Help!*
and frantic, when I opened my door.

I remember her shoulders
in the faded towel I found

before she put on my blue sweats
and white T-shirt. *Call 911*

please, she said.
When the officer arrived

I said, *I found her there after the—*
But she said,

No, that wasn't what
happened.

What must be valued
I'm learning,

in clarity and in error,
are spaces

where
feelings are held.

Here—in a poem?
And elsewhere

Vigil

As I pedal down these streets, space and joy becoming one
        wind at our backs, striped awnings up and down Main;

I cycle fast, pant leg cuffed, calf streaked with grease, threading our way through
        locked traffic, past the canal, around Belle Isle;

I glide toward the glint of light that shimmers off the reflector on her
        rusted ten-speed,

then follow her to a spot along the James, where we trapeze across railroad tracks,
        where to blink might mean to lose foothold.

Here she points across the river to an osprey nest.

Tufts of straw jut out of a distant utility tower.
        Silhouettes of birds circle overhead,

eyeing us, eyeing their nests.

       ★

I need to tell you about the seeing that goes on between two people,
        around two people. Not the touching. The watchfulness.

This is not just about love, though I love her as much now as then.
        It's that she's always looking out.

If I follow the dotted lines of her gazes she's looking out at some thing
        just out of range:

a river otter surfacing beneath a boat dock,
        a damselfly dipping below a waterline,

a wasp out a tiny hole in a hollow gall,
        that wasp lifting its legs.

      ★

Years ago, I followed the gaze of a kid, looking at me through
        a mirror in a public restroom in a park in California.

I knew by the duration of her looking that I was already a spot in the glass,
        a small detour in her life that she was building a barricade against.

As she pressed her nose to the glass, each exhale fogged the pane.
        I knew her. I was her. I left her.

      ★

I am a woman who forgets sometimes that she is a woman.
        So I always slip my shoes off and knock, at least three times

before crossing a threshold, before presuming I'm welcome here.

      ★

Out the window of a speeding car a man yells, *Dyke.* And a silence bristles
        between us,

hot ash about to blow across a paper city.
        If you love someone, you must be the guardian of their solitude.

Not that she ever needed me to guard her. Her biceps are firm when she folds me over in the dark.

Desire among Sparrows

I like to wake up early by myself
and wander out the door as echoes do
then perch to dream with a bowl of cereal
and think without order about this world

inside then out, this world as small enough
to lose inside the liner of going-out jeans,
the ones without a pocket left anymore.
Out here I'm the Chief of Sparrow Police

when I note the elbow shapes of half-torn sage.
I like to think the thief just needed a nest.
My nest had pale blue sheets, and then alone
again, it had the old polka-dot pair

that finally wore out beneath my feet,
a hole that spread whenever socks rustled.
I changed them out for paisley ones, until
someone new thought I ought to have a spare.

These ones are orange. Like rust. Or like the shade
the day lilies might turn next spring, if the bulbs
take root in rain. Enough about flowers
and birds, but never enough about sheets.

James River

You are a wren scavenging for
    the husks of beetles.
        I am a trout poking

through river rocks, the head of
    a copperhead slipping past,
        the shadow of what you asked for

turning to husk. I am an open
    parachute, breeze billowing through.
        You are a wren scavenging

for the husks of beetles.
    Now, I am flotsam
        poking through river rocks—

the detached head of
    a copperhead snagged on rocks.
        During recess, I remember

the parachute in my hands
    an open shadow
        breeze billowing through

when everyone pulled
    the chute upward to run beneath.
        I was flotsam

moving through river rocks,
    a ghost net emerging.
        The parachute faded

indigo was sweaty in my hands.
     Tucked beneath, one might
          feel whole when everyone

pulled the chute upward
     to run beneath.
          Tell me: How cold is

the fluid beneath your kneecaps?
     A ghost net emerging.
          How red is the air

beneath your fingernails?
     Tucked beneath
          one might feel whole.

How remote is any
     one appendage
          from the other?

How cold is the skin
     above your kneecaps?
          Don't tell me the body won't

turn on you. I am the air
     red beneath your fingernails,
          a trout disappearing into

river rocks, close as any one
     appendage from
          the other, the shadow of what

you asked for
     turning to husk.

Your mouth is stretched panther–wide
        in the last good photo taken of you,

the creases in your forehead symptomatic
        of some form of inscrutable effort. You're on a stage

in a bar singing a song you can't remember,
        insides burning with inflammatory denial.

You can't believe love left you. And yet,
        you do happy better than any drag you've seen in weeks,

gleaming like a gem on Liberace's finger,
        shameless in the wan karaoke light.

Regardless of how you feel inside, Diane Arbus said,
        always try to look like a winner.

It seems to you there are infinite medals
        and behind the medals, no other world.

No landing like Mary Lou Retton
        arms flung back in a USA leotard

after perfect executions on the floor mat. If only
        you could be that headstrong

as you sprint toward the mic.
        Here on a hollow stage

your fingers skim the frets of an air guitar.
        Once a friend warned,

Every relationship is a dress rehearsal for the next.
What are you wearing?

A dogged smile, a jersey at the end of a dirty match,
too blinded by the strobe in the dive bar

to register the blur of
your teammates' faces.

Your figure is a cold ornament
embossed with leaves.

(Are they fearful or joyous?)
as you point and sing:

Do you wanna touch me? There. Where? There. Yeah.
Touch your skull,

the mounted antlers of a red stag.
The first meaning of trophy:

a tree made of someone else's
armor, spears, quivers, flags,

stolen breastplate,
a monument to pieces.

Tonight at a party we will say farewell
to a close friend's breasts, top surgery for months
she's saved for. Bundled close on a back step,
we wave a Bic lighter and burn her bra.
At first struggling to catch nylon aflame,
in awe we watch as all but the sheer black
underwire melts before forming a deep
quiet hole in the snow.

                      Sometimes the page
too goes quiet, a body that we've stopped
speaking with, a chest out of which music
will come if she's a drum flattened tight, if she's
a canvas pulled across a frame, a field
where curves don't show, exhalation without air.
Then this off-pitch soprano steals through.

Then this off-pitch soprano steals through
a crack that's lit. A scarlet gap between
loose teeth. Interior trill. We're rustling open.
Out of a prohibited body why
long for melody? Just a thrust of air,
a little space with which to make this thistling ·
sound, stretch of atmosphere to piss through when
you're scared shitless. *Little sister, the sky
is falling and I don't mind, I don't mind,*
a line a girl, a prophet half my age,
told me to listen for one summer when
I was gutless, a big-mouthed carp that drank
down liters of algae, silt, fragile shale
while black-winged ospreys plummeted from above.

While black-winged ospreys plummeted from above,
we were born beneath. You know what I mean?
I'll tell you what the girls who never love
us back taught me: The strain within will tune
the torqued pitch. In 1902 the last
castrato sang "Ave Maria."
His voice—a bifurcated swell. So pure
a lady screams with ecstasy, *Voce
Bianco!* Breath control. Hold each note. Extend
the timbre. Pump the chest, that balloon room,
and lift pink lips, chin so soft and beardless,
a flutter, a flourish, a cry stretching beyond
its range, cruising through four octaves, a warbler,
a starling with supernatural restraint.

A starling with supernatural restraint,
a tender glissando on a scratched LP,
his flute could speak catbird and hermit thrush.
It was the year a war occurred or troops
were sent while homicide statistics rose;
I stopped teaching to walk out, my arms linked
to my students' to show a mayor who didn't
show. Seven hundred youth leaned on adults
who leaned back. We had lost another life
to a bullet in the Fillmore, Sunnyside,
the Tenderloin. To love without resource
or peace. When words were noise, a jazz cut was steel.
I listened for Dolphy's pipes in the pitch dark:
A far cry. Epistrophy. A refusal.

A far cry. Epistrophy. A refusal.
A nightingale is recorded in a field
where finally we meet to touch and sleep.
A nightingale attests
as bombers buzz and whir
overhead en route to raid.
We meet under cover of brush and dust.
We meet to revise what we heard.
The year I can't tell you. The future restages
the past. Palindrome we can't resolve.
But the coded trill, a fever ascending,
a Markov chain, discrete equation,
generative pulse, sweet arrest,
bronchial junction, harmonic jam.

Bronchial junction, harmonic jam,
her disco dancing shatters laser light.
Her rock rap screamed through a plastic bullhorn
could save my life. Now trauma is a remix,
a beat played back, a circadian pulse you can't shake,
inherent in the meter we might speak,
so with accompaniment I choose to heal
at a show where every body that I press against
lip syncs: *I've got post-binary gender chores* . . .
I've got to move. Oh, got to move. This box
is least insufferable when I can feel
your anger crystallize a few inches away,
see revolutions in your hips and fists.
I need a crown to have this dance interlude.

I need a crown to have this dance interlude
or more than one. Heating flapjacks you re-
read "Danse Russe," where a man alone and naked
invents a ballet swinging his shirt around
his head. Today you're a dandier nude
in argyle socks and not lonely as you
slide down the hall echoing girly tunes
through a mop handle: *You make me feel like . . .*
She-bop doo wop . . . an original, domestic
butch. The landlord is looking through
the mini-blinds. Perched on a sycamore,
a yellow-throated warbler measures your
schisms, fault lines, your taciturn vibrato.
Tonight, as one crowd, we will bridge this choir.

Late Bloom

The name of the spotted apple
on the leafy floor in the woods

outside the white-walled bedroom
where the FM stereo was always

tuned to the same country
station my girl crush loved

was gall, name for an outgrowth,
a shell withering under leaf rot

near a spot where the surprise lilies
might remember, might

forget to bloom. Touch a weevil
and it will fall, legs and antennae tucked.

Blink and the artic fox becomes snow.
The gecko, toes spread wide

on a tree trunk, passes for lichen.
Of all the ways a creature can conceal itself,

I must have relied on denial.
There were the Confederate bumper stickers,

pressures from seniors to tailgate,
the spindly legs of a freshman

scissoring out of a trash can,
how just the smell of Old Spice

could make my muscles contract
like a moth, wings folded

the color of a dead leaf in October.
So that she might hear her favorite song

my voice would drop, and if the DJ answered
I would be Tim, Charlie, Luke, Jason

every name but my own.
Truer than gold.

Wasn't I the stripe in a tiger's eye?
The dapple in the flanks of an Appaloosa?

In daylight, how could I possibly explain:
A heart hunting after a body?

Notes

Many facts about animals that appear in these poems came from *Biological Exuberance: Animal Homosexuality and Natural Diversity* by Bruce Bagemihl.

"Dappled Things:" Lines by Gerard Manley Hopkins are echoed throughout from "Pied Beauty," "I Wake and Feel the Fell of Dark, Not Day," and a journal entry from March 1871. Gentle Hop was a nickname given to Hopkins by his Jesuit peers.

The now extinct female gastric-brooding frog could transform her stomach into a womb. A mother would swallow her own eggs. After several weeks of metamorphosis, she would birth fully formed froglets out of her mouth.

"In Full Velvet": Some of the phrases I use to describe velvet-horn deer were found on hunters' message boards.

Monique Wittig and Sande Zeig define "cyprine" as "a love secretion" in *Lesbian Peoples: Materials for a Dictionary*.

"Elegy at Twice the Speed of Sound": In his keynote address at the 1992 OutWrite conference, Melvin Dixon said, "I'll be somewhere listening for my name." He died that same year.

"There Are New Worlds": Stephen Gordon is the protagonist of Radclyffe Hall's novel *The Well of Loneliness*, published in 1928.

"Gay Marriage Poem": The etymological attention I give to the word "wedlock" is based on Elizabeth Freeman's discussion of the word in her preface to *The Wedding Complex*.

"Vigil": The penultimate stanza invokes a letter by Rilke to Emanuel von Bodman on togetherness between two people: "Therefore this too must be the standard for rejection or choice: whether one is willing to stand guard over the solitude of a person and whether one is inclined to set this same person at the gate of one's own solitude . . ."

"Desire among Sparrows": This poem was written after "Desire Under the Pines" by Tim Dlugos and borrows its first line.

"Aria": References are made to the following songs and recordings: "Kimberly" by Patti Smith, "Ave Maria" as sung by Alessandro Moreschi, Eric Dolphy's version of "Epistrophy," the BBC live broadcast of nightingales from May 19, 1942, "Fake French" by Le Tigre, Aretha Franklin's version of "(You Make Me Feel Like A) Natural Woman," and "She Bop" by Cyndi Lauper. "Danse Russe" is a poem by William Carlos Williams.

The work of Larry Levis also spurred a few of these poems. The boots in "Souvenirs" are his—I saw them on display in 2010 at *Larry Levis: A Celebration* at Virginia Commonwealth University. Rereading "There Are Two Worlds" led me to write "There Are New Worlds"—my poem began as a conversation with his, but after subsequent revisions, it veered away. While drafting "Elegy at Twice the Speed of Sound," I spent time with "At the Grave of My Guardian Angel: St. Louis Cemetery, New Orleans," a syntactic guide, which taught me ways to move through time and space.

Acknowledgments

Many thanks to the editors and staff at the publications in which these poems, some in alternative versions, first appeared: *Beloit Poetry Journal* ("Aria"); *Blackbird* ("Severe" and "Elegy at Twice the Speed of Sound"); *The Collagist* ("Tail"); *Cream City Review* ("Folsom Street Fairytale" and "Gay Marriage Poem"); *Los Angeles Review of Books Quarterly Journal* ("Dappled Things"); *New England Review* ("In Full Velvet"); *Paris Review Online* ("Souvenirs"); *Phantom* ("The Bus Ride" and "Victory"); *Poem-a-Day, Poets.org* ("In the Dream"); *The Southern Review* ("Pine Street Barbershop"); *Twelfth House* ("There Are New Worlds"); *Waxwing* ("Little Apophat" and "Dorothy's Trash").

"Aria" was reprinted in *The Best American Poetry 2012* (Scribner). "Ladies' Arm Wrestling Match at the Blue Moon Diner" was printed in *Best New Poets 2008* (Samovar Press/*Meridian*). "James River," "Late Bloom," and "Vigil" were printed and "Tail" was reprinted in *Troubling the Line: Trans and Genderqueer Poetry and Poetics* (Nightboat Books).

The completion of this book was greatly supported by the Blue Mountain Center, Bread Loaf Writers' Conference, Friends of Writers, Kimmel Harding Nelson Center for the Arts, The Pittsburgh Foundation, Virginia Center for the Creative Arts, and the Whiting Foundation. I am immensely grateful to Sarah Gorham, Kristen Radtke, and the staff at Sarabande Books for their editorial assistance and vision.

Thank you for your guidance Debra Allbery, Rick Barot, Jan Beatty, Gabrielle Calvocoressi, Jennifer Grotz, Mary Leader, Ellen Bryant Voigt, and C. Dale Young. Thank you to my students who are also some of my greatest teachers. Thank you Jeff Oaks and Geeta Kothari for holding me accountable. Thank you old and new friends for the conversations, adventures, and support that emboldened so many of these poems: Annemarie Brown, Veronica Fitzpatrick, Liz Ahl, Sarah Rosenthal, Ari Banias, Alina Del Pino, Molly Minturn, Charlottesville Lady Arm Wrestlers, Cupid Ojala, Nichole Faina, David

Francis, Brenna Munro, the UVA Young Writers Workshop community, Ray Daniels, Goldie Goldbloom, Mary Jo Thompson, Matthew Olzmann, Olivia Kate Cerrone, Emilia Phillips, Ben Strader, Alexis Canoy, Joseph Hall, Jasmine Hearn, Adil Mansoor, Luke Niebler, Nick Liadis, Rayden Sorock, O.E. Zelmanovich, Paul Kruse, Jessica Heathcote, Maybe Jairan Sadeghi, Cara Erskine, and Bekhyon Yim. Lastly, thank you Jennifer Chang, Margaree Little, Soham Patel, and Brooke Wyatt for being my best and closest readers.

Jenny Johnson's poems have appeared in *The Best American Poetry 2012*, *New England Review*, *Troubling the Line: Trans & Genderqueer Poetry & Poetics*, and elsewhere. Her many honors include a 2015 Whiting Award and a 2016-17 Hodder Fellowship at Princeton University. After earning a BA/MT in English Education from the University of Virginia, she taught public school for several years in San Francisco, and she spent ten summers on the staff of the UVA Young Writer's Workshop. She earned an MFA in Poetry from Warren Wilson College. She teaches at the University of Pittsburgh and at the Rainier Writing Workshop, Pacific Lutheran University's low-residency MFA program.

SARABANDE BOOKS is a nonprofit literary press located in Louisville, KY, and Brooklyn, NY. Founded in 1994 to champion poetry, short fiction, and essay, we are committed to creating lasting editions that honor exceptional writing. For more information, please visit sarabandebooks.org.